T0020192

QUEENS OF THE ANIMAL UNIVERSE

ELEPHANT COWS
Heads of the Herd

by Maivboon Sang

PEBBLE
a capstone imprint

Published by Pebble, an imprint of Capstone
1710 Roe Crest Drive, North Mankato, Minnesota 56003
capstonepub.com

Copyright © 2023 by Capstone. All rights reserved. No part of this publication may be reproduced in whole or in part, or stored in a retrieval system, or transmitted in any form or by any means, electronic, mechanical, photocopying, recording, or otherwise, without written permission of the publisher.

Library of Congress Cataloging-in-Publication Data is available on the Library of Congress website
ISBN: 9781666343021 (hardcover)
ISBN: 9781666343083 (paperback)
ISBN: 9781666343144 (ebook PDF)

Summary: A lion sneaks slowly toward a herd of elephants. The herd's female leader sees the big cat. She charges the lion and it runs away. Females are the leaders of an elephant herd. They protect the herd, lead it to food sources, and care for young. Take a look at elephants and the important roles cows play to ensure the herd's survival.

Editorial Credits
Editor: Carrie Sheely; Designer: Bobbie Nuytten; Media Researcher: Morgan Walters; Production Specialist: Polly Fisher

Image Credits
Capstone Press, 7; Getty Images: Elena Kabenkina, 25; Shutterstock: Alexandree, Cover, Andrzej Kubik, 22, Atosan, 8, Carcharadon, 15, BrightRainbow, (dots background) design element, Ercan Uc, 12, Henk Bogaard, 5, jo Crebbin, 9, Johan Swanepoel, 21, John Michael Vosloo, 23, JONATHAN PLEDGER, 11, 17, 20, M.INTAKUM, 29, markdescande, 19, Michael Potter11, 10, Mikhail Kolesnikov, 13, Nicola_K_photos, 18, Quinton Meyer ZA, 14, Sergey Uryadnikov, 6, Stu Porter, 27, Volodymyr Burdiak, 28, WinWin artlab, (crowns) design element

All internet sites appearing in back matter were available and accurate when this book was sent to press.

Printed and bound in the USA.   4882

Table of Contents

African Elephants Rule! 4

Meet the African Elephant................. 6

Elephant Bodies 10

Elephant Herds.....................16

Working Together........................... 22

Beyond the Herd.....................24

Amazing Elephant Facts...............28

Glossary.....................30

Read More.....................31

Internet Sites.....................31

Index 32

Words in **bold** are in the glossary.

African Elephants Rule!

For animals that live in groups, males are often the leaders. They're usually bigger and stronger than females. But it's not always size that matters in a leader.

Elephants live in groups called **herds**. Female elephants, or cows, lead herds by their smarts! Let's meet these great animal rulers.

Elephant herds are made up of mostly female elephants and their young.

Meet the African Elephant

There are two kinds of African elephants. Bush elephants live in grassy **savannas**. They are found south of the Sahara Desert. Forest elephants live in the forests of Central and West Africa.

Forest elephants stand near a forest in west-central Africa.

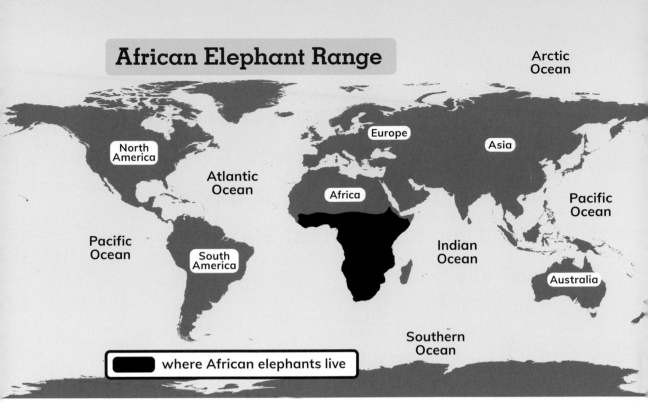

African Elephant Range

Arctic Ocean

Europe

Asia

North America

Atlantic Ocean

Africa

Pacific Ocean

Pacific Ocean

South America

Indian Ocean

Australia

Southern Ocean

■ where African elephants live

Only about 415,000 African elephants are left in the wild. They are in danger of becoming **extinct**. Some people hunt elephants for their **tusks**. The tusks have a valuable material called ivory in them. The hunting has caused elephant numbers to go down.

Elephant herds stay on the move. They tromp through forests. They splash through **swamps**. In a year, a herd can travel almost 300 miles (483 kilometers)!

Elephants spend time cooling off in water.

Elephants are plant eaters. They eat grass, leaves, roots, fruit, and bark. They eat small trees too. They spend an average of 16 hours a day eating.

Elephants eat a large variety of plants.

Elephant Bodies

African elephants are the biggest animals that live on land. They can weigh up to 7 tons. They can be as tall as 13 feet (4 meters). Males are larger than females.

Elephants walk about 15 miles (24 km) a day.

Elephants have small eyes for their large size. They can't see well far away. But they can see movement well. Elephants can also see all around them.

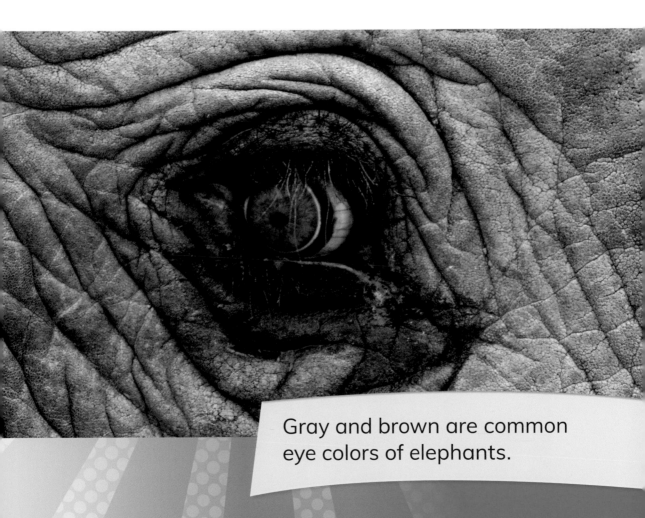

Gray and brown are common eye colors of elephants.

African elephants have big ears. Their ears can be up to 5 feet (1.5 m) wide and 6 feet (1.8 m) long. Elephants hear well. They hear sounds that people can't. Their ears also help keep them cool. On very hot days, elephants quickly flap their ears to cool down.

When elephants flap their ears, the moving air carries heat away from their bodies.

Elephants have big noses too! An elephant's nose is called a trunk. It is about 7 feet (2.1 m) long. It has more than 40,000 muscles. Elephants use their trunks to drink water and grab food. They use it to spray water too.

An elephant's nostrils are at the tip of its trunk.

Sniff! An elephant uses its trunk to sniff the ground and the air. Elephants have a great sense of smell. It is five times stronger than people's.

Elephants smell the air as they travel. It helps them know if dangerous animals are in the area.

Tusks can be 6 feet (1.8 m) long. Bush elephants have tusks that curve outward. Forest elephants have straighter tusks that point down. Tusks help elephants dig, strip bark from trees, and defend themselves. Male elephants will use their tusks in fights with other males.

Two male elephants fight.

Elephant Herds

Elephant cows live in herds their whole lives. One female is the leader, or **matriarch**. She is often the oldest herd member. A herd includes the matriarch's sisters, daughters, and their young, or calves.

Male elephants leave the herd when they're 10 to 19 years old. They then travel around alone. Sometimes they form small herds.

A matriarch leads her herd through a national park in South Africa.

Elephants have different ways of communicating. Elephants make many sounds, including trumpets, grunts, and rumbles. They may trumpet to scare off a **predator**. An elephant calf may rumble to tell its mother it is hungry.

Elephant mothers are protective of their calves.

Herd members use touch to communicate too. A mother will check if her calf is nearby by swatting her tail. If the calf isn't nearby, she will look around for it. Elephants may greet each other by wrapping their trunks together.

Scientists think elephants twist their trunks together to show affection.

Elephants have very good memories. Even if they are apart for years, elephants can recognize each other.

Elephants form close bonds with the members of their herd.

A matriarch can remember the paths the herd has taken. When food and water are hard to find, she leads the herd to where they can be located.

It can get very hot in Africa. Finding water is very important for elephants.

Working Together

Elephant cows help one another. If an elephant gets stuck in mud, others will help get it out. Other elephants will feed a herd member that cannot feed itself. If a mother elephant dies, others will care for her calf. Older mothers help inexperienced mothers protect their calves.

An elephant cow checks on a calf that is in mud.

When an elephant mother gives birth, other elephants often gather around her in a circle. This keeps her safe from attacking animals.

Elephant cows work together to care for calves.

Beyond the Herd

Elephants don't just help their herds survive. They help other animals too.

Munch! Crunch! A forest elephant herd gobbles up small trees and other plants. These elephants make paths for smaller animals. They clear plants. Then new ones can grow.

Bush elephants dig into a dry riverbank with their tusks. There has been no rain. Animals all over are thirsty. The elephants dig and dig. Finally, they find water. Now all the animals can drink.

A forest elephant munches on a tree branch.

Elephants help keep the savanna open. They tear trees out of the ground and eat them. This helps animals that depend on the grassy, open areas for food.

When elephants eat fruit, the seeds pass through their bodies. The seeds come out when elephants poop. New plants grow from the seeds.

African elephants can live up to 70 years. But without adult females, a herd would have a hard time surviving. Female elephants are amazing animal leaders!

An elephant mother leads her calf through tall grass.

Amazing Elephant Facts

Elephants can be left or right-tusked like people are left or right-handed.

Elephants can recognize themselves in a mirror. This is something very few animals can do.

An elephant's brain can weigh 9 to 13 pounds (4 to 6 kg).

An elephant is pregnant for 22 months.

Elephants can eat up to 300 pounds (136 kg) of food a day.

Elephants poop about 2,000 pounds (907 kg) a week!

Elephants can show many emotions, such as joy, sadness, and fear. People who work with elephants learn to recognize and understand their emotions.

Elephants can sense sounds through their feet. If it rains far away from the herd, elephants will travel toward the rain because they can feel thunder through the ground.

Glossary

extinct (ik-STINGKT)—no longer living; an extinct animal is one that has died out, with no more of its kind

herd (HURD)—a large group of animals that lives or moves together

matriarch (MAY-tree-ark)—a female elephant that leads the herd

predator (PRED-uh-tur)—an animal that hunts other animals for food

savanna (suh-VAN-uh)—a flat, grassy area of land with few or no trees

swamp (SWOMP)—wet, spongy ground often partly covered by water

tusk (TUHSK)—a very long, pointed tooth that sticks out of an animal's mouth when it is closed

Read More

Pringle, Laurence. *Elephants!: Strange and Wonderful.* New York: Boyds Mill Press, 2021.

Rustad, Martha E. H. *All About Baby African Elephants.* North Mankato, MN: Capstone, 2022.

Smalls, June. *She Leads: The Elephant Matriarch.* Sanger: Familius, 2020.

Internet Sites

Britannica Kids: Elephant
kids.britannica.com/kids/article/elephant/353093

National Geographic Kids: African Elephant
kids.nationalgeographic.com/animals/mammals/facts/african-elephant

San Diego Zoo Wildlife Explorers: African Elephant
sdzwildlifeexplorers.org/animals/african-elephant

Index

brains, 28
bush elephants, 6, 15, 24

calves, 16, 18, 19, 22, 23, 27
communication, 18, 19

ears, 12
emotions, 29
eyes, 11

food, 9, 13, 21, 26, 29
forest elephants, 6, 15, 24, 25

herds, 4, 5, 8, 16, 17, 19, 20, 21, 22, 24, 26, 29
hunting, 7

males, 4, 10, 15, 16
matriarchs, 16, 17, 21
memory, 20, 21

plants, 9, 24, 26
   trees, 9, 15, 24, 25, 26

Sahara Desert, 6
savannas, 6, 26
seeds, 26
size, 10
smelling, 14
sounds, 12, 18

trunks, 13, 14, 19
tusks, 7, 15, 24, 28

water, 8, 13, 21, 24

Author Biography

Maivboon Sang is a writer of short stories and nonfiction. When not writing, she enjoys working her way through pastry cookbooks. She lives in Minnesota with her husband who believes she makes too many desserts.